Crowned In Melanin

by

Lady Syren

2023

For media, review, or permission requests, please email
LadySyrenSpeaks@gmail.com

ISBN: 979-8-9886874-1-2

Logo concept & design by Vee Allen
Logo designed rendered by Logo Angel
Front & back cover design rendered by Nick Austin
Back cover photo credit to Kahleel Frazier

You are MELANIN & MAGIC

CONTENTS

Acknowledgements

Welp, if anyone besides myself is reading this, that means I've really gone and done it. I published my first book of poetry. Finally! I couldn't be more grateful to those blessing me with their time, presence, energy, and of course, funds. I couldn't be more grateful to YOU. If I literally listed every name, and the level of impact, of each person who has contributed to my motivation in finishing this project, I'd have a totally separate book of just those. If you saw me, spoke to me, captured a pic, recorded a poem, and or messaged me in the month of June, **I'm especially talking to you**. The amount of affirmation I have been blessed with, in this month alone, has been extremely soul nourishing. But to everyone, your kind words, enjoyment of my work, attending my events, liking, commenting, and SHARING my social media content, your overall support, has lent itself to pushing me to finish. It has all served as a gentle hushing to calm my nerves. A loving whisper in my ear that kept telling me, "You got this!"

I want to give a special shout out and thank you to my daughter Kai. Who danced around our living room and celebrated when she discovered I was working on a book! I am certain she will indeed be a published author at a much younger age than I. So baby girl, on that day, we will dance around the living room together.

To my love, Nicholas, thank you for keeping me in check and accountable to the goals and deadlines I set for myself.

Introduction

I am a black woman
With a black pen
I want to bleed out my experience
On these pages in black ink

Crowned in Melanin has been an idea for quite some time now. Only having been given a name and careful intention a little over two years ago. This is my love letter to blackness. The culture. The plight, and the privilege. A reflection on growing up as a black woman in a country that works overtime attempting to devalue who I am at its core. I am a woman who's taken many detours in learning to love herself, and her skin. As an artist, it has taken even longer to be secure in valuing my voice and finding necessity in being heard. So, I welcome you to embark on my poetical celebration, and in some ways, a reimagining in what it means to be unapologetically black. I pray you enjoy the journey as much as I did.

"Blessed with the gift of melanin
in her skin
She's a FORCE to be reckoned with!"

Queen and Crowned

There is no jewel encrusted structure on my head
So, they wonder…
WHY do I call myself a queen?

Well, the answer isn't too complicated
But it does require you to LOOK, where the eyes can't see
That's because it's
Living
Breathing
and ever changing!

More than hair
The crown be my spirit
See, my kinks get a lil extra knotty
Extra springy when it coil
Roots naturally reaching out to graze the sun
So, I gotta give 'em their space to grow
Don't need a heavy accessory
I've learned that that's just added weight
Because heavy is the head
As the saying goes

Nol need to be adorned in metal
When God has laced gold all through my melanin
Baby
I am the crown
The treasure
The gift
Royalty in my lineage
Divine energy my essence
Nothing more malleable than the black woman
And, in my eyes…

There's no one more precious

Gold's the only metal that can be stretched to the thinnest point of
visibility
Much like a black girl's dreams
Or worse
Her being
Barley teetering on the edges of existence
Bejeweled in
No
Coated
24 karats of melanin
I have
Been dented by the oppression
Bent and made to fold over myself
I have been crushed
I have been stretched
And forced inwards all over again
I have been smoothed
Etched
Shaped
Never broken
I was designed for this

Society says I'm painted as a target
But no
To be crowned in Melanin
Is to know the hue of my glow is beautiful
Rooted in the radiant color of rebellion
Resiliency
Resplendent reciprocity

No one struggles

Or fights
Or cries
Like, the black woman
I know this melanin is blessed!
Because no one loves like she
Queen and crown
She....
Is me

If I asked you, what is the greatest love story ever told?
What would you say?

Now, if I asked you, what's the scariest horror story ever told?
...

What if I told you the two were one in the same?!
That the scariest, and most beautiful love story ever told, is black
people finding, loving, and losing each other generation, after
generation...

A Love Reincarnated
is a Trauma Revisited

Traveling through history, and loving you through time
In fact, WE STARTED time… it began with us
Now maybe we can't say for certain
Whether or not this love affair started in a garden
But there must've have been a fall from grace in our linage
Somewhere we were cast out of humanity's gates
Forced to endure an eternity of star-crossed fates
Over, and over again by translucent hands
Our trauma reincarnated, looming large and inescapable
The reincarnation of black love, under white supremacy?
It is as incredible… as it is infuriating
It is as warily indescribable, as it is inundating
Because who would choose to keep loving, in a world that insists
on hating us?
Because we know there's more to life than just death
Know there's more to strife than just heart-breaking lessons
But I'll never learn mine when it comes to you
I loved you from the moment I saw you
As I do every time
I KNEW I wanted to procreate & continue our blood line
But we went to war before the bridal tribute with a neighboring
faction, and lost
You were a causality in this dispute over land
So, I never felt the warmth of your hand
Anywhere but on the graze of my cheek
When you bid me goodbye
I prayed, chanted, and danced well into the night
as is our tradition
In hopes that the Gods would return you to me
But they didn't

I would die, and live, and die again, several times over
Before I found you again
Still proud, still strong, still fighting for our people
As you had been since the age of 15 when you began to
acknowledge and publicly support the NAACP
But that charming smile hadn't graced mine eyes
Until we were 20
Quickened Heart beats be the funeral precession that plays as I see
you walking toward me
How much love will this lifetime, grant us this time
You were heavy into your work for CORE
Congress of Racial Equality here in meridian
And that didn't leave much time for courting
You'd taken several freedom ride trips and I waited in fear
But rejoiced each time you'd climb back off that caravan
Your embrace dissipated all my angst and
for a moment
There were no civil right movement
Just us
But fate always catches up
And one fretful night
In the wake of your voter registration rallies
You, Goodman, and Schwerner were arrested
For a supposed traffic violation
Although released the same night
The white of your colleague's skin couldn't make you right
Or worthy of getting out of Mississippi alive
Deemed guilty by two carloads of the Klan
Disappeared you all in an instant
They each garnered one bullet to the heart
But you, the only black man there, earned three
It would be 44 days until they found your bodies
And I would go 40 more without sleep

And more than half a century before our souls met again

This time
We grew up together as kids
I guess we knew it then
Our mothers certainly made enough jokes at our expense
But we fought it nonetheless
Until we couldn't
Reunited in college
And finally gave in to that ancestral pulling
Like a magnets
The expanse of your aura sung to me
I, 24 and you 25
8 months post marriage
We were blessed with the gift of Son-shine
Oh, how your excitement exploded when I told you
You took me in your arms
and we danced to music that wasn't playing
And we'd repeat this ritual again and again
In the months to come
Until my feet were just too swollen to two step
It was almost time to welcome your name's sake into our lives
As he'd already consumed a great deal of our hearts
But when the time came
Something…was off
You weren't there
Both our mother's stood by me in your stead
But you, baby, are my strength
How was I supposed to do this
Without YOU holding my hand
More than the birth plan
The *life's* plan was to do *this* together
Where are you?!

I want to be angry
But something in me screams
It's happened again
No!
I concentrate on pushing
The pain of my heart *cracking open* in my chest
Rivaling the contractions
And then… he emerges at 6:02
Quiet at first. then loud as can be
Your eyes
Your ears
Your lips
All appear to have been shrunken
And placed on his tiny little face

Later I would learn mistaken identity was the case
Shots fired at 5:49
Pronounced DOA at 6:01p
Does the story behind the bullets even matter any more?!
It's like I spend my whole life longing for you
Looking for you
And letting my desires pass me by
Until I find you
And
I *know* it's you
I feel it's you
My spirit never lies
You amplify and elevate my divinity like no other man could have
Heartbeat quickens as it only does for you
And you are mine
But even when I have you
I don't get to keep you
Because they keep snatching you away

Maybe I shouldn't care no more.
Maybe I don't wanna love no more.
Maybe I don't wanna live no more.
Not if being ALIVE is but a tease
Not if every time I find you and love you,
I fear for you
And lose you to their hate
It's embedded in my DNA
The gift and curse of loving and birthing black Gods
So
No matter how many ways this life seeks to strip our time away
I will always muster up a seed of strength to love you again
Because I see you out here surviving
And I'm trying to survive too
So baby please, keep seeking and hold on to me
And I'll keep waiting, and hold on to you

"They call us the minority, but there is nothing MINOR about my people!"

The Assassination of Black Divinity

Curse across this country for any who bare a resemblance to me
But the trick is, there's no removing this skin
Many shades of melanin, hair of all different textures
And Eye reckon this evil runs centuries deep
Amulets of protections forged by our ancestors
Long ago stolen, broken, hidden, forgotten, now rare
Leaving us susceptible to the evil stares of our enemies
Maleficent glares baring tangible daggers that dig, twist, and
wound deep
Now isn't that a ghastly scare ghoulish enough to incite blood
curdling screams
But...not as much as the fact that
This soil's made fruitful (rich) by nutrients leached (decapitated)
from decaying black bodies
Black bodies
Who blood paved the streets in a home
Where we could never belong
Ripped away from ancient teachings meant to keep our mind,
body, and spirits strong
It's a systematic dismantling of our defenses
That leave us destroyed and defenseless
It's more than skin deep
And there's no beauty in this transatlantic tragedy
Or the reality that we're a long way from home
Don't even recognize mother Africa as such
So, she weeps, soil so red, she bleeds when she sees
They've stolen the glint of hope from our eyes
Mined the diamonds from our smile
They've drilled & extracted black gold from our very souls
So, hallows eve is said to be the devil's day
But here in America, real devils?

Don't bother to wear masks anyway
Instead, they'd like to disguise us
Draw us as unrecognizable caricatures

But the picture you're looking at
Has been hung by another...
You're viewing a canvas painted by them
Whitewashed!
 Brush strokes that paint a picture of discord
Lost women
Absentee fathers
And an overall unintelligent species
Stripped of our pride and robbed of our culture
Decimated and broken down
They pick over us like vultures
When are we going to wake up?
My people, we've been asleep
Eyes wide open to the bling, mind closed to our history
Hearts closed to humanity; spirits closed off to our destiny
Where are we going? And What are we doing??
They call us the minority, but there is NOTHING minor about my
people
Our culture
Our traditions
The immeasurable contributions to society
And while they attempt to condense our historical events to Their
lil 28 days
To that?

I say they're crazy! Our blood sweat and tears are in the foundation of this country, America exist due to slavery
So by all means, don't segregate "black history!"
My history is your history, and our history is this history, and dammit that's American history!
And schoolbooks recount stories of blacks being set free, supposedly
But there's far too great a number still stuck in a shackled mentality.
They're trapped in a subconscious loop that's programmed to degrade, alienate, abandon, and shoot!
* Boom *
They're aiming at us in every direction and if history has been teaching us any lesson, is that we're greater together than we are apart
So when are we gonna start getting it together and going at this thing called life together

"The lessons given in this life, do not get easier.
We simply (or rather complexly) become better equipped at
pushing forward.
And
More strategic on whom and *what* we allow to teach us said
lessons."

Let Me Let You In On This Secret

YOU
Are more than what the world has allowed you to be
MORE valuable than what others have led you to believe
YOU
Are Bigger than the four walls of the box they've tried to contain
your ambitions in
And far more worthy than any one disappointment
...even your own
Overly critical
Fixated on the negative
At times, unforgiving
That. Is. The human condition.
To be tough and unrelenting in the face things that make us
uncomfortable
But GROWTH is an *uncomfortable* thing
Let me let you in, on this blessing
The favor in getting taller
Stronger
Bigger
The gift in growing UP
Is that we do it slowly
Sooo gradually
And physically (for the most part)
Without pain
Our cells duplicated rapidly...stretching across our frame...and
again, we feel nothing (generally)
Only notice it when it is already upon us
Made evident by exclaims of
'my look how much you've grown'
Or the fact that our clothes are too short and too tight
Still

16

We are not so lucky when it comes to emotional & spiritual growth
It is quick, intense, and hard to bear
Internal growth at times happens against our will
Beyond our learning
And severely tests our threshold for pain

Pssst...
Let me let you in, on this healing
Love you through the growing pains of your spirit
There is no over the counter or prescription
Only *giving in* to the lesson
And moving
Preferably forward
But sometimes ping ponging
Amidst the woulda, shoulda, could ofs
And forgiveness
For those who've hurt us
Flat out tried to break us
But most often...for ourselves
Uncomfortable, is never the destination
Only the means
By which we are made to shift
Of getting to the other side
Of where and who we're supposed to be

Let me let you in on this secret....
You. Can. Survive it.

To be crowned in melanin
Is to acknowledge the plight of our social standing and treatment.
But
To delight in the blessing of being black, all the same.
It is
To know more than one side of our history.
To deconstruct, understand, and pass on the lessons learned, the
same way we pass down/teach all the line dances we plan to do, at
this proverbial cookout we're always joking about!

When it comes to the "cookout?"
If you know. You know.

Formaldehyde

I can almost see it
F- Fr- Frr

It's almost in reach
But, f-f-

Freedom!
Freedom, isn't a word I can EASILY speak
Not in all aspects
Not truly
Not where I'm from
America, the one with three K's
Cause trust, that ain't no C
Unless? We're speaking
On the color they see
Not where I be
Philly
Not as she
Me
Not with the skin I'm in
Black
I spend every waking moment, sipping on formaldehyde
Because from the moment we're born, we're destined to die
Whole world's out here trying to speed up the timeline
More than proverbial, literal fingers clutch my neck
Stay robbing me of breath
Of faith
Of love
Of energy
Of life & liberty, well before our last *breathe in* exhale
Embalming us with injustices
Because we all know it's JUST. US.

Thick ass liquid of bullshit
So here we are stiff
Ice in our veins and hearts be congealed
You Want to speak on suppression?
And I'm not talking about votes
Suppression of human rights
Erasure of cultural pride
Economic depression
Leading to the decimation of goals
They're killing us hard out here
It's a constant Destruction of souls
How we unwanted guest in our own damn home?
Trying to reinforce our foundation
But stepping up to lead, gets harder
Activists turned martyrs?!
We cry
We yell
We raise hell
Then barter
Just to end up, right back where we started
There's not much living in this life
Yet often, we're smiling through it
Just a bunch of walking stiffs
Fire of our wills turned Rigor mortis
Stillborn spirits struggling to seek a sense of peace
Moving in a country
Too dull
Too Deaf
And too damn blind
To appreciate my gifts
Our presence? Is nothing short of a blessing!
But we're brow beaten into thinking we're insignificant

Still view us as $\frac{3}{5}$

As stated in the constitution

Which is why the scales of justice are persistently imbalanced

And don't even get me started on their incessant appropriation

Too many attempts to duplicate

But they couldn't begin to imitate *this*

And you know what?

I guess that's why they hate us so much

How we're your biggest inspiration?!

Yet regarded as your biggest threat?!

And there it is…

Go on and take it in

The sight of America's ejaculation

Forced to put my mouth to it's tip and slurp down every sip

And if the images of pale white dick makes you uncomfortable

How much more are we?

To know that our perps are literally untouchable

But this?

This just how these mutha-f**kas get off

But, not as much, as when these violent pigs get OFF

Always erect for moving black targets

Just ready and waiting to shoot their off

Enough bodies stretched forth to pave new black roads

Enough blood spilled to paint every city's halls RED

But shhhhh. STOP complaining

Be quiet

Stop! We like to shoot

So remain silent

Forever

Since the beginning of time

They've been telling us

They're the protectors of everyone but US

They're only here to Serve the racist's agenda
So,

'just lie down and let us do our part
Don't *you people* like walking 'round casket sharp
anyway?!'
Well, we're just here to get you fitted
Tailor made & suited
So here
Just guzzle down this CUP of mortuary juices!'
So… as I was saying
Every. Damn. Day.
I'm sipping on formaldehyde
Because from the moment we're born
We're destined to die
And if you're born in black skin?
You could spend a great deal of what little time we have
Here on this earth
Wondering…why?

The pain inflicted on our bodies
Is rivaled only
By the pain inflicted on our hearts.
How we still manage to respond with such a force, that
is NOT rooted in revenge.
But instead rooted in LOVE, still amazes me.

Black love is unique in its ability to endure AND empower!

Haiku

Faith is love AND works

Spirituality goes

Beyond religion

To know me in real life, or if you see me often
You'll eventually pick up on the fact that I love to dress up!
But my absolute favorite fit, is a whole lot of self-love,
accessorized with confidence!

Honey Coated Melanin

Covered in satisfaction
Drinking in what little beauty
This life has to offer
Delectable essence
That emerges from when the struggle meets peace
When spiritual torments are released
Sweetest taste of divinity
Seeping from my pores
At the revelation of my inner being
Firmly planting peaceful kisses
Upon the parts the world deems dark
Pleasantly licking picturesque design of my future
Dancing to hopeful rhythms of my heart

Therefore…
I'm here for
Filling cups to the brim
Until my joy runneth over
And oozes over the edge and slides down my finger tips
Sipping on drips of pleasant from my unexpected
And rolling 'em across my tongue

I look up…and wonder
When did you get here?
Where do you hail from?
How long have you been watching
This succulent
Consumption

The Struggle gripped my chin
Fortitude kissed my lips
And
Revolution *danced* on my tongue

I Said My Queens

I Said My QUEENS
Yeah?!
We looking, sounding, writing, so good today
Wellll, a Queen of the pen, be stunting *every* day
I said, *every* day

Even if we don't always feel like it
Even when we aren't feeling like ourselves
Don't always feel like putting on a show
Yet
We must strut on
As the saying goes
No rest for the weary
And it's scary just how worn
We allow ourselves to get
Because our kids need this
Or hubby needs that
What is work life balance
When we're mentally on the clock
All hours into the night
Budgeting bills
Reviewing grocery lists
There's *always* something to do
An elderly parent to check on
A home to make
A friend to console
Or a wash day to *literally*
Set aside an entire day for
But WAIT
There's more

All the things that go unsaid
All of the internal battles
We're struggling to win
All the alley-oops our confidence must do
To keep our hearts afloat
All the doubts we hurdle
Only to fail clearing the pit
Those first few moments of panic
Setting in when we find ourselves falling
But sometimes
Falling is really flying
We just haven't spread our wings yet
Doesn't negate that we're still soaring
Albeit it honestly hovering just above depression
And sometimes we aren't hovering,
Heads barely above water
but treading
The fact of the matter is, we're still pushing
Praying **U**ntil **S**omething **H**appens
But still getting up, going out
and making sure that *something* happens
And it just so happens
That we look good while doing it
Most days
Because

The magical thing about Black Girls
Is rarely do we ever look like, what we've been through
Rarely do we ever crumble, the way society expects
No. Wants
No. Demands
Us too!
We're beautiful

At every stage of our healing
Especially, when we're feeling
Anything but attractive, so to speak
Even when we don't wish to illuminate our reflection
Our true strength lies in our eyes
We're prone to seeing in the dark
And *that's* that shine
Of a black girl's glow!
That's that gift
Of a black girl's soul

So
Here's to all the black girls
Black women
Black beings, crushing their goals
Crushing their fears and overcoming trauma
Every. Damn. Day!
But Sis, slow down when you need to
Be it breath or break
Please, do tend to you
Braid or twist your tresses
Fluff your fro
Or massage your scalp
You're allowed more than a moment
Your efforts are NOT in vain
And Your pain won't last forever
Although time is relative

Just remember
YOU are fierce, capable, and intelligent too
Give yourself the space to be vulnerable
To make AND learn from your mistakes
You are allowed to be human
Even if your shirts are really just capes
Parading as everyday clothing
I see you Queen
Even when you don't see yourself
I love you
Even when your actions make you question
If you love yourself
You got this
WE got this if need be
Just lean on me
And together we'll keep stunting, glowing, and winning
And Passing the game on down to the next

I pray that you heal
from all the things
you haven't felt **safe enough** to discuss yet!

Inside These Bags

I don't pop tags
Never have
Grew up too poor
Material things I owned too far and few
Emptiness often consumed every state of my being
Sometimes staring into the bottom of the bag
to reignite the pain, was the only thing that gave life meaning
Licking the tips of my fingers to grasp at the crumbs left
in balled up bags of Stroehmann
Because little bro should have the bread
The last slice left
But, I had THREE younger siblings
So I searched the cupboards for remnants of stale cereal
and relinquished that too
Then, let the weight of emotional baggage sit upon my gut
in hopes of suffocating the snarling teeth attempting to growl their
way through my abdomen
Traveled deep into the well of my emotional pain in hopes of
drowning
I no longer physically desired to be present
I'd much rather leave this little girl's bleak story unspoken
Cause I had a childhood that broke me down & ripped me open
Took suture needles to my skin and low key enjoyed
the agony of my wounds closing
Sewing up the craters that were blasted into me at such a young
age
I could recount stories that were more than skimmed knees
Enduring terror designed to emotionally skin me alive
Blessed to know that as I aged, my will to live
Outweighed my yearning to die!
Most days…

Procrastination likely saved me in so many ways
If I'm being honest
I've started many goodbye letters in my head
Yet never picked up a pen
Too many people I'd likely write "Fuck you!"
A few I love and would want to give answers too
Just thinking about it had me mentally fatigued
Tried my best to inhale the confidence
And exhale my insecurities

Sometimes your head is high
But your spirit is low
Sometimes Your smile is wide
Even when your tears haven't even begun to dry
So don't feel bad for me
You see I wrote this poem
Because I've been working on me, & loving on me 34yrs strong
I knew I wanted to
I needed to
My last resort was to do better
Because life's a cold hearted, unforgiving BITCH, who'll destroy
you if you let her
So if/when you hear me pen stories that give a mere glimpse of my
tragedies
Just know I'm following up
Recounting my victories in every letter
Written for, by, or about Vaniece

Cause I'm still a beast b
Still beautiful after everything sent to break me
Still pushing forward despite the weight of everything
sent to bury me
Still loving unjaded despite experiencing this world's hatred
Still counting my blessings no matter the attempts to block my
vision
Still praying
Still mothering
Still pushing my pen
Still living

And that's half the battle!

Trigger Warning:

The next two poems offer a very small snippet of my experience with childhood sexual abuse, emotional manipulation, and trauma.

"What happens in this house, stays in this house!"
Is perhaps the most dangerous lie and demand we could
force upon our children.
The stories may decay within those four walls,
but the trauma lives on in every person who crosses the threshold
....and manifests itself accordingly.

Black IS beautiful...but, the <u>culture</u> can be toxic at times.

Small Silence

I don't remember how young I was
But I do recall learning it the hard way
As many children in restrictive
and or dangerous households often do

That
Little bodies are not built to carry 'free' things
Not speech
Not expression
Not Autonomy
Nor will

They are built
…or broken
To merely carry what the adults have chosen to give them
BUT
Little bodies are juuust big enough to house secrets
The nooks and crannies of vulnerable bodies present all the right
places to tuck lies in
If you're *depraved* enough

That's the thing about depravity
It is pervasive
Piercing
And all too *silent*
About as quiet as tiny little voices dwarfed in fear
Choke on what predators force them to swallow
Fearful little bodies longing to sing freedom songs
Not simply to be heard
But to be protected

My freedom doesn't sing
I was never taught the words
My freedom doesn't dance
I haven't the rhythm
My freedom...doesn't play
Anything

Grief plucked my heartstrings until they were broken
Shame hammered into my truth until I went deaf
Tightened my tongue to roof of my mouth
Until it melted into hard palette
and no longer exists
For predators make percussion of lil bodies
Beating. Drumming.
Drumming. Beating.
Beating so loudly
On little bodies too young to sound off verbally
Too quiet to get the attention of someone who'll give a damn
At least gain the ear of someone
who could recognize the muffled sounds of abuse

Little known
Well known
But *often* ignored fact...

My girlhood died in the hands of a man my mother loved
Strangled out in a grip that stole my innocence's last breath
Buried it
Beneath an addict's sick ambition
So, so, sooo heavy
Too heavy to move
Too heavy to run
Too heavy to fight back

Little bodies aren't built to bare THAT weight in any sense
My body interred my voice alongside my innocence
While my mother's neglect left it's grave unmarked
So…
Here lies nothing
May it **Rest In Poetry**
Because…
We don't talk about it

I affirm, that I am not my trauma
I affirm that this poem is NOT my trauma
I affirm that this glimpse into my life is just that. A glimpse
I confirm that this happened to me throughout my young life
AND
I survived!
I affirm that these are not open wounds I press against paper
I affirm that I am safe
I affirm that I am healed
I affirm that I live accordingly

MaMa Said

Mama said, I'm a liar
Mama said, maybe I didn't want her happy
Mama said there's no way I was telling the truth
Because
  'Why would my grown ass man want anything to do with you?!'
Mama said
        'Oh, What, you have nothing to say?'

I was 8
I was confused
I was in need of saving
So, I hesitantly and desperately told my truth
Mama said, it was alright. That it'd be ok
Mama said, she was here for me
Mama said, that she loves me
Mama looked at me
And then she said, if you're serious
Give me your hand
She gripped it tight, snatching a bible up too
Pulled us both across the room
Forced my hand upon it and then
Mama said,
        'You wouldn't lie to GOD would you?!'
You know what it would mean to swear a lie upon this book
Don't you?!
You know where bad
I mean fast
I mean lying ass lil girls go, don't you?!

Mama said all I had to do was tell her again
Exactly how I told it to my friend
Exactly what I had said to the fam
Exactly what I had already disheartened-ly divulged to her
Again

The cops were now here
Mama said, we had to have our stories straight
Because her boyfriend's, no this man's LIFE was in the balance
Mama walked away, leaving me in silence
Soaked in my own tears
Tears that for some reason, I was too scared to wipe away
Maybe if mama just saw my face
I'm her big girl who never cries
These weren't lies, this was my truth
The truth
Popular saying is there's always three sides
But there's only has one version
When it comes to speaking true right?
Right??

Mama never came back for me while speaking to the police
Mama spoke for me
Mama told my story
No. Told *A* story for me
Mama said, he'd have to leave
I felt myself slowly giving into some…relief?
I willed myself to hesitantly breathe, again
And then
                    I heard mama quietly say…
                    She doesn't believe me

Self Care:

When it comes to the things I have control over, nothing is done by accident. I approach my writing with great intentions. That's for everything! From journaling, notes to self, and all the works I have no plans of ever sharing with another soul.

To date, my biological mother (and other family members) still carry the belief that I made it up. That somehow, a friend who was spending the night during one of mother's drunken all-nighters at the bar, and I concocted a story of molestation out of boredom (or fun?).
When the fact of the matter is, that little girl was the first person to tell me that a grown man was not supposed to put his hands on me that way, or interact with me sexually.

I had gone my whole little life never being given permission to have autonomy of my own being. A little girl, only a bit older than myself, had taught me an invaluable lesson. One that allowed me to recognize signs of grooming when it almost happened again.

A lesson that I took great care to be very deliberate in instilling into my own daughter.

One I pray continues to protect her.

I am more than the sum of my pain
I am worthy of healing
I am worthy of triumph
I am worthy of stability, consistency, and longevity
I am worthy of love
I am worthy and capable of giving love
I am free to choose my path
I release any thoughts that hinder my progress
I *choose* progress
No matter how slow the process
I *choose* progress
I *choose* me

UGLY

Yellow.
White girl.
Oh, you think you all that?
Ugly bitch!

The first time I was ever called ugly?
Not even sure I was old enough to comprehend
All that matters is, I believed it
When's the last time I've been called, pretty?
I'm guessing words of affirmation only come in
houses or homes that little **black** girls are loved in
Healthy affection? Only occurs in homes
that little **black** girls are embraced in
And the grips I grappled with
Only sought to invoke harm
So, I merely existed betwixt four walls
Like the 4 letters of such a simple word
Ugly that is…
Existed in the mouths of those far less attractive
Rolled off their tongues with ease
Yet, nothing was easy about taking their hits
Not into my auditory canal verbally
Or upon my chin physically
Cause sticks and stones
The old adage, it is said
But if words could never hurt
Why'd they weigh so heavy in my chest
Why'd they replay so often
Keeping me awake every night
As I laid in my bed
Asking
Praying
Begging
For god to bless me
Bless me in some way that would allow them to see

46

Me, for me
Or just leave me the hell alone
I admit I got picked on, a lot
But there was no safe haven to offer a pick me up
A word of advice
But words, are just words, right?

And Ugly is a 4 lettered one
That can so accurately describe so many things
None of them being something as shallow
as a person's appearance
But do you know what is?

Being motherless while residing in the same domicile
Where your mother is
but not actually living
Nor receiving proper nourishment
Not for my body or my emotional development
When I think of the depths of my most unsightly scars
All the memories flood in
As triggering reminders that UGLY
Is my mother's passive comment about how
"They" gonna lovvve you!
That left me confused about who "they" were
And…what did it mean to be bow legged?
Then she filled in the blanks
About how men love bow legged women
But ain't I…a kid?

In her eyes
This is what made me attractive
Between my legs is where my value is
In *her* eyes this made me pretty
For a long time
I existed in the gray area of one's compliments
Left myself with little to no love
And my self-assertions were mute

Amorphous and colorless
A shapeless cloudy mass of nothing
That allowed me to amass a pile of sorrows
I kept swept beneath my feelings
Until another's insult instigated an itch
That would crawl up from under epidermis
And tickled it's way across raised hairs on my skin
And despite it be longed healed over
I find myself scratching again

Beneath the surface of all the hateful things they said
Beyond all the frivolous labels they forced upon me
Because People everywhere are constantly projecting their
insecurities
But I am NO a screen
Just more confident and capable of refracting their dim lights

Look at me now
I've transmuted all of this ugly
Into a beautiful display
Yeah I did it
Uprooted the definition with no alibi

You damn right
And you'd wanna be this too

U. G. L. Y.
Uniquely Gifted. Loving Yourself!

Tainted thoughts, leave bitter notes on the tongue.
Resentment can cancer the mind
and
clinging to negative energy
dims & sours the feeling of being alive.

Bitter Tastes Better

Sometimes
Bitter tastes better

When it serves as reminder
That this *life*
Ain't always sweet
A reset to the palette
When
I've been consuming sugar too long

Forgetting that the soothing texture of *honey*
Is just a ploy to ease the lies down my throat
Hopeful side of me, so desperate for nutrients
And apparently *dumb enough*
to beg for a second helping
Consuming convoluted tales
That plate my feelings with contrition

But no repentance for dessert
Just a side of depression
To trigger my tears
Spoon them into a small dish
A delightful array of condiments
For bullshit to dip its fingers in
I stare… as it licks the satisfaction
of my brokenness off the tips
And *suddenly*
I'm
STUCK

Watching in awe
Like
How can this entity be so full?
When I'm so *damn* empty
Like
How could it dance about my kitchen??
When I'm so *damn* angry!

How can it continuously shovel out
more than I could ever stomach
Yet
I keep dropping in weight
When am I gonna push my chair far away from this table?

But I haven't the energy
Because everything I'm eating
Lacks sustenance
And this thing's
A *bottomless pit*
It's, it's, it's
Been feeding off of ME this whole time
Siphoning off my strength
Emaciating me from the inside
It likes the taste of flesh
And thrives off my doubt
My complacency
My fear
My inability to forgive too
And I invited it in

Since, I've never liked the taste of salt
It didn't mix well with my ambitions
Tiny granules of disappointments
Have turned in to a mound of sorrows
This gluttonous redundancy
Bubbles up like acid reflux
Now?
I'm.
Stuck.
In a cycle where I keep *stuffing*
My face
But the only thing that grows?
Is this
Bitter
Bitter
Taste
Sometimes, bitter, tastes better

In the moment...
But
It doesn't sustain

Dear reader

These poems aren't free!

Not for the obvious reason, that they are in this book, which will eventually be sold.
But in the way that it costs us, the artist, *something* every time we pick apart our pain or document our healing.

These poems aren't free!

On & On

Check it
Like
sing song
Oneee
Twooo
Threeee

The world keeps turning
Oh, what a day
What a dayyy
What a dayyyy

The man that knows something, knows that he knows nothing at all
Does it seem colder in your Summertime, and hotter in your fall
Oooh
On and on
and on and on

This
Song keeps playing for me
Oooh, on & on
And on and on

This
Pain keeps on unfolding for me

Line by line, these, pages keep on turning for me
And I find myself wondering, why am I here?
Do I genuinely belong in this space I've created?
OR
Have I, too long neglected my inspiration in favor
of less cluttered, head spaces?

My ambitions? Often play tug of war with my fears
I don't wanna go there, up there, the ladder of success?!
What if I'm afraid of heights?

Sometimes
I lay beneath these sheets crumpled up within my thoughts
Stripped down to lines of nothing, but my truth and vulnerabilities
As a dope poet
My, earthly King once said, **these poems aren't free!**
Do you know how it feels, do you grasp what it means?
To take the dull point of a pen to your proverbial wrists
And *bleed* upon pristine pages lyrically
Are you even listening to the small voice that escapes my throat?
My written essence pouring from betwixt my lips
Will it even have anywhere to go?
Or will they fall upon death ears and evaporate into nothingness
Nothing is more egregious than shrinking yourself
Or dimming your *own* glow
So you, my dear audience
Bear no responsibilities here
Although
Cleverly conveyed criticisms come covertly concealed as
compliments
Confession
NO ONE
Has been more violent with me, than I have been to myself
Acknowledging I've outgrown certain people and things
But simply loosening the seams to continue *shoving* myself into
obscure places
Because there's simply less judgment, in the shadows

Recurring question of ponderance
I wonder if I'm strong enough

Strong enough to live LOUDLY
When it comes to legacy, the last thing I'd want, is to leave quietly
So I keep writing
Understanding the plight of the poet is to stare directly into the
depth of something so terrifyingly ugly and recast it as something
beautiful
But ....
There is no beauty to be found in child molestation
Tragic untimely deaths
My mother's crack addiction
OR my suicide attempts
Some traumas need a lot more than a little poetical lipstick
Because some ish is just...,sad
But traumatic events aren't the things I carry *with* me
They happened *to* me
They aren't the present reality that I'm living
And **I affirm, that I am more than the sum of my pain!**
Crying is a cathartic act and a spiritual cleansing
My tears
fall upon death bed in maternity ward
for I, am reborn again
It's a release of the stress pulling me asunder
separating me from my peace
When reunited with my inner calm?
I, am made whole again
Putting myself back together again
Over & over again consistently
And it is only by the grace of GOD, that I can
Goooo
On and on
And on and on
My faith keeps moving like a rolling stooone!

The MIND is the hardest thing to train

and

Our SPIRITS are the heaviest thing to lift.

Of Shadows & Light

Sometimes, you remain in the dark so long
It becomes easier and easier to forget just how beautiful you are
When you immerse yourself in unyielding shades of black & gray
It becomes harder to keep our minds from being consumed too

Life will come at you swift, and blunt
Instruments that sing of our demise in the form of those we trust
Realize
They will lie to you
More than speak untruths
They will scar you
Batter your energy
Disfigure your being!
Not just physically
At times, you are dealt wounds so deep it cuts through your soul
So, you retreat into obscurity, in an effort to heal
Withdrawing from the world around you and close your eyes
because you'd rather not see the damage

We're afraid of shining light on even the good fragments of
ourselves
For fear of also seeing the parts of us that are broken
Misshapen
Or even just slightly tattered.

You do not have to sacrifice the bit of you that remains intact to
cover up those vulnerable places
Resort to yanking every star from your very own sky
…endlessly night
Who'd want to wish upon a glint of hope, when

With every disappointment
Another shovel of dirt is thrown into the hole you're standing in
With every failed accomplishment
Dark thoughts moves you to have a hand in burying the bruises
on your body
But, look closely
They are a part of you.
Embedded in *your* skin

A mental grave is a cold, dirty, disorienting space to be in
But <u>nobody</u> is coming to dig you out from beneath the weight of
your *own* mind
So, whenever you're able to open your eyes just enough
to let a little light in
Open wide and let it shine!
Because all of you deserves to be seen and loved

To succumb to the darkness indefinitely?
Is to is lay down and be buried
YOU are worth more than self-imposed eulogies
YOU deserve to feel all of life's sensations
Although
You prefer numbness over feelings…

I know

It is easier to seek the safety in loneliness
But to be alone
Is to be without challenge
And to be without growth
How do you appreciate the warmth of the sun and everything that
thrives in it?
If you're never thrown into darkness

It is unfathomably cruel to think what your brain can do to you
for no apparent reason at all
But
Your wellbeing is a collection of things all coming together
And not necessarily all at once
Number one being the *desire* to survive

It is a fact of physics that in the presence of light
Darkness isn't completely vanquished
BUT severely diminished
The key to this is preserving the beacon of your consciousness
Grounding a higher power at the center of your spirit
So the fire of *your will* has to burn brighter than the pain that
crowds you
And it is true
That sometimes, an illness requires medicine
But what if it's just your *thoughts* that are sick?

When you began to evaluate the situation
You may see you have a bigger hand in remedying it

The mental battles are the hardest to win
The mind is the hardest thing to train
But it's a <u>muscle</u> nonetheless
You reinforce its' strength with each decision you make to try
again!
I choose to bask in the sun because my glow will always be bigger
than the shadows
Please
Love yourself into your healing.
You deserve that much

The mind is indeed difficult to train. But have you ever had to contend with your heart?!
That, is the real beast!

Fallen

Have you ever witnessed a star being consumed in a fell swoop?
A soul's jaw unhinged to expose all 9 realms of *hunger*
Makes gourmet meal of genesis
An insatiable inferno which intensifies the instant temptation
tangos at the tip of its tongue

See,
"Self dignity" lacks the necessary rhythm to entice a taste
Not enough sway in its hips to seduce invitation
Abandonment casts a flirtatious glance
Giggles in uncertainty
Flashes white wings of innocence
And pays for her own ticket down into the belly of blasphemy with
the shining gold halos
that adorn her consciousness
Beck-on-ing baccalaureate bestow the heart with several degrees of
dunce
Damnation. Awaits.
Don't do it. *Don't* do it
Immaculate blaze of trumpets
Sounds off to Announce God's presence *and* your undoing
Antiquated testaments mere thunder bolts of reprimand to dodge
When the most beautiful creation makes dance floor out of embers
that fall from the heavens as their desires *crack- open* sky
Swim through 52 shades of midnight
Transfigure atmosphere to canvas
Carving their initials into each cloud
And cutting away strings of divinity
That tie her back to **truth**
Displaced GOD energy *surges. Spilling. Plunging.*
Collapsing in on itself!

Breaking waves on the shore that meets on *his* arms
Soaking
Chastity is wet with its own lust
Stirs in Belted frustrations
And
Deception drinks each distinguished drop of discernment dripped
during descent
Knocked off axis with the trajectory and impact of a comet
shooting down her spine
Collides with reality
Blows a crater into expectations
Makes new orbit of his body
and is introduced to **everything** and *nothing*
She grabs hold of absurdity
Rides it
Fucks it
On every piece of anticipated memory
In every space
Of each realm
She goes back and rips all the belongings of common sense out of
the closet
And allows her peace to be penetrated there too
Again. And again
Sensation in her pores be tiny mouths
licking their lips
Tiny mouths that fervently moan
As fused energy culminates into chorus
Reduced to a simple repeated sentiment
Because it doesn't want to leave a hint of respect in any of it's
corners
In unison they harmonize mournful dirges of,
"I don't care. I don't care!"
I don't care if they can hear me

I don't care if prides other victims can smell me on him next
Make them wait
Let them wait for me to coat him in my tears
And my cum
And every lesson my creator instilled in me
WAIT
Let this moment be mine

So...
Let the moment be hers
If eros be an eater of galaxies
But he emanates the moon and sun
Then let her explode.
Climatic consequence of orgasmic supernova burns enough to
brand his name
On her tongue
So he's the only language she knows
Because she can't see the cosmos for all the stars in his promises
Or the milky way between her thighs
Interstellar leap from seraph to mortality
Have you ever witnessed a celestial being give itself to gravity
The texture of falling is gritty
It's jagged and sharp
Ties shredded flesh into ribbons of regret
Thick enough to stifle sounds of self-love
And intuition
Thick and entangled enough to hang you from
Thicker than the strings he lead her from
But not enough to fly
So this
Is where glory goes dim
And there is no miracle of resurrection
.....to be had

My spirit sings grief
Like…
The gospel.
Bellows out hallelujahs
With a whole lot of praise
And…
Just a hint of sadness.

Didn't You know

Didn't You know?
That there are parts of herself she finds too hideous to be shown?
The parts of her that *stayed* in that house
Chained to the stipulation, that what happened there, SHOULD
Forbidden from escaping those four walls
OR being freed from her two lips

She has no desire to shine light, or love, or healing really
On all the swapped out and misshapen parts of herself she's
exchanged with the world
The tattered and torn pieces of her joy
she's *snatched* from rough hands
Or
The vacancies
Of where she's carved out pieces of heart
Gifting them to lovers
But was never *given* any love
The same ones who kissed her lips *so sweetly*
But *chewed* on her smile!

Didn't you know?!
That the pursuit of pliant pretty pink flesh is often times
A violent act
There's a trail of teeth in carnage's wake
Yet she maintains her ability to speak!
So, forgive her if she brandishes a deformed tongue
For she too
Has *impaled* it
Clamping down on all things she "shouldn't" say
Tied it up with all the NOs jumbled in her cheeks

Didn't you know?
That there are parts of her deemed too *offensive* to be heard?!
So she EATS that pain
And swallows the fluid
So the first time a woman sees blood
Isn't in the seat of her pants

It is in her SPIT

Starts as a trickle…
You should smile more
Then a small gush!
When she learns
She is both responsible for HER actions and the man's
A red flood ensues
The first time a woman loses her autonomy
And realizes… it may not be her last

Always bending, and biting, and tearing
But to not sever such a delicate muscle
Is got damn magic trick
And it's not even her best one
Just the one that could possibly keep her most safe

Did you know
That there are parts of herself too scary to venture into alone
There are times when she may place her happiness
at the feet of those
Who know not what it means to handle her with care
She doesn't actually plan to fall in love with the demon
She's just attracted to his sense of direction
THEY know their way around this hell
She doesn't willingly get dragged *through it*

She's just holding on
Praying that the next corner he turns is the way out

For women who've been consumed
and abruptly ejected from the bowels?!
They, are a formidable thing
Even they find grace
Blown into the arms of those who've been here and felt this before

Dressed in white
With kinky curly locs that adorn their crown like melanated halos
Beautifully unscathed on the surface, it seems
But these disfigured souls, tell a different kind of story
For they *too*
Have scrubbed the stench of Sulphur's smell off their skin
and lived to reclaim their glow

Rooted in the medicinal vines of sisterhood
They
Be a dispensary of dope conversations
Laced full of wisdom and patience
Filtered With Warm vibrations
that puff up deflated confidence *and* hearts
They reaffirm to her
Although Betrayal's *sticky* in the chest
Icky alongside rib cage
Leaves the *dank* smell of heartbreak
So they sniff her coming from a mile away
Process however you deem reasonable to weed out deception
Make it a chronic habit
Roll up his broken promises
Light up all the potential you saw in him
And *all* your plans

Sister, my sista!
PUT IT to the PAPER
Let your tears *burn*
And play those memories *loud*
Inhale the vapors of all the fucks you gave?!
breathe
And *exhale that bitch!*

Despite swollen tongues being weighted with the names of people
she should of *cursed*
But prayed for and blessed with absolution instead

That's the whole point!

Even disfigured tongues recount her truth
Can you hear it?
Or do you feel too convicted
to listen?!

One day

She looked in the mirror

Saw each, and every flaw

Smiled. And said…

My god, you're beautiful!

You

I'm going to take my time with you
Like a glass of water, I'll slowly sip
Trying hard to resist my urge to gulp you
I'll crack you open, & lick the sweetest parts of you
I'll travel the length of your depths
Into the darkest of your shadows
There isn't a corner of your universe
the light of my love won't attempt to go
Invade all the nooks of your crannies too
There isn't an ounce of you I wouldn't consume
I'll Lick the sweat of your inspiration
Drink the essence of your happiness
I'll massage away your stress
Until the beauty of being melts again
Release the tension, then go back in
Like, I want more of it
I'll crave you in all forms, even just a hint
You're a natural aphrodisiac
In case no one's said it yet
And I'm a glutton for your energy
I even want you intravenously
You're just that dope
Hum of your spirit be internal periscopes
Each perspective serves up new views
I wanna peel you back. Delve into each layer
Each depth ever more delightful
Voice often quiet
Pics hella dark
But ya vibe be hella loud
Make sure we're looking in the mirror
When we recite this piece out loud

I've often said

"If you want to see a unique and beautiful magic trick?

Watch a black woman do her hair!"

An Ode to Big Bette`
(aka My Hair)

I was never taught to love my tresses appropriately
Introduced and addicted to that creamy crack by the age of 10
Meant for follicle digestion AND to eat away at our confidence
Because never forget that everything about the black experience
Should be toned down, stripped of color and served
With a lot less seasoning
Don't want to offend their vision
Or upset their lil bellies with our spice
But what about the narrative we're serving ourselves?

Honestly…
My hair enters a room, before I
And like most little black girls
I've been conditioned to see my hair
More akin to a shield
Rather than a crown
It's been a rather entangled journey to
refrain from using my curls as camouflage
To stop chemically beating, blowing, and singing my kinks
into submission
Cause Girls like me, with all melanated shades like mine
Weren't meant to blend in
I was born to stand up and stand OUT
Like the hair on my head
Black girl magic just seems to naturally
Go against so many European standards of beauty

But isn't that obvious?
There's a little **rebellion** in my DNA
Every coil in each strand

Represents 1 black woman that's been silenced
Shunned
Or shamed

My hair is representation
Presents as a show piece
When my fro is fluffed just right
A show stopper for any looky lous that dare to reach
If I had a dollar for every time
I've looked a white woman DEAD in her eyes
Had to stop myself from popping a hand
She be just short of pulling back a nub

These strands have removed many teeth from many a comb
Bristles from brushes
Behinds from chairs
And eyes from their sockets
Hell
I've even removed a few Dominican stylist from their patience
When they could no longer hide the grunts
Detangling my hair at their wash stations
Like you didn't set up shop in a community full of beautiful black
women
Like you aren't swimming in a sea of black hair
Be it growing by the root
Or attached to a track
But still had the nerve to cock your head to side and ask
"Why you hair get so nappy like that"

blank stare

Won't even dignify that with an answer!

MAYBE the way my hair ceases up beneath the water
Is attributed to my ancestors
Wary hands that became a chain link of KNOTS
LOC'D in prayer
Begging!
No!
Please!
Don't throw us in there

From head to toe
Root to tip
We need the appropriate amount
And the right kind of moisture to remain malleable
So, what?!
The bonds of my keratin don't like being WET
But it be necessary for cleansing
Unlike all your questions
About why this
Or why that
Listen. **I'm black.**
Bu- bu- but
Your long hair, and your light skin??
I SAID
I'm black
Black, black, blackity black!
I've got good hair cause there's African in my blood

Like the all the natural products used
to condition my fibers so soft and shiny
I'm a concoction of my ancestry
And therefore
I'm a walking, talking, hair flipping contradiction
To everything you THOUGHT we should be

Like, despite all the inherited stressors
And perfectly planned suppression
I'm surpassing hair and financial goals
Got you trying to figure out how I'm still thriving
How my edges stay laid and keep growing
Cause baby, I'm bold
Bold like, rocking a wash n go to all my interviews
Brave too
Brave like, taking a red-hot comb to the dome
My hair
Like my vibe and volume of my voice
It's boisterous!
Unapologetic for space we take
Although, I do feel a little bad
When we're blocking your way
But greatness is to be celebrated
NOT contained
So
The next time you fix your lips to criticize
The length, style, color, or manageability of a black girl's hair
STOP
Cause if it's not a compliment?
WE.   DON'T.   CARE.

And baby?
THAT'S on hair!

Do you enjoy the sound of wind chimes?
Melodic and peaceful to some.
Jarring and unsettling (for some unknown reason) to others.
But ain't that just like being black in America?
Feeling calm in the blessings bestowed on your life, being butted
up against a deliberate rage that's constantly bubbling beneath…

a smile.

Wind Chimes

Their melody, comes to me at a distance
Nestles into the rustling synchronicity of the leaves
And their tune *dances* about the air
And begins…discordantly tap dancing on my spirit
Would it surprise you to find
That I *don't care* for their vibrations
I find myself warding off the desire to *flinch*
Every time when I hear their sound
The tingling…of wind chimes
A sound most find calming and beautiful
Barrages my ears, more like a *ringing*
Perhaps? It reminds me of the faint sound… of chains
And the Ancestral sprits, rooted in my being, *cringe* at the clanging
Clanging against boats
Clanging against cages
Maybe…even each other
The dull *ting* of a thud against black skin covered in sweat
as they crashed into one another
*heart beating *
Panicked heartbeats serve as a bass line
To the melodic *sting* of metal
Kissing metal
As ill-fated black souls kissed death
Unknowing and mildly
I hear them …wind chimes. Lilting in the branches
Bathing in beams of warmth being emitted from blue skies
The glisten of the sun, off their shiny metal sides?
Reminds me of the light shimmering off the surface of the water
Long after the splash of struggles have dissipated
After all of the *bodies* have long settled at the *bottom* of the ocean
The *bodies* we'll never see

Improper burials besiege my memories
Somewhere. Somehow.
But the recollection doesn't belong to *me*

Do you ever wonder if their souls have found... rest ?
Or do they *too* become submerged in sea floor sediment
Are they still chained there being held captive in the after life
Waiting to be born *free* in the next

Does their consciousness, float along the breeze
Do you think they meet in the wind?
That blows through the trees of which, their relatives were hung
All the ones who took the trip and *made it*, but never *made it*

The twinkling chimes of softness
Sounds so soothing to others
But it sounds like cold laughter to me
Shrill
Their haunting melodies echoes in my mind
Like, blood soaked key notes in highest pitch of their frequencies
It sounds like *music* to you
But it sounds like mass murder and mayhem to me!
I- I- I'm sorry...
You just wanna hang wind chimes
And I'm *clearly* managing my triggers
So, buy and display them, if you *must*
If you absolutely INSIST on getting wind chimes
please consider ones that are wooden?
And I *promise* NOT to give you a trauma poem
about the floorboards, of slave ships

At the intersection of race, class, and gender oppression, lies very little room to be soft.
To be, "free."
The strong black women trope isn't a character aspiration for most black women.

Simply a necessity.

The Strong Black Woman

Strong.
    Black.
        Woman.
Pillar of her community
Ride or die for her King
To be **crowned** in this supposed strength
Is to be shackled to an identity
That doesn't always suit us
But it keeps us suited up in an emotional armor
Always ready to fight the good fight

To be of this touted slogan
Is to be on the front lines of every major
movement that propels society forward
But seldom does society ever move for us
It seems the ranks are thinned when it comes to marching
Advocating for and saying *her* name
Whomever she is
Wherever she was
Or whatever form of her black or brown face
The world always has a way of dismissing
Their women warriors
And many aren't even full-fledged women yet
But they are indeed battle tested
The only thing quicker than a fast lil girl
Is the adultification of her innocence
There is no slow walking into our plight
We're rarely ever gifted a smooth and
Clearly defined rate of transition
Often, we're thrusted into our womanhood

Like the fowl to the wolf
Or a flame to the wind

To be preyed upon
Or snuffed out!
THIS is the harsh reality when you are born
Of these three things
Strong.
    Black.
       Woman,
So, to make it well into adulthood
Is to bear battle scars that are *soul* deep
To tear hands and heart wrestling your way
From betwixt the jaws of death!
Leaving a blood trail that makes it easy
For our demons to find us again
All while smiling
Hashtag, *grin* and *bear* it

The toxicity of this tag line
Toes the line of a placated necessity
A stereotyped caricature of what it means
To be enveloped in a black cape
An overhyped ideal
That we fly from place to place
Problem to problem
To save any and every situation

While that BGM surely packs a *punch*
Who's caping for us?!
To be super and sub-human, all at once?
Is to be fetishized and forgotten

We are placed on pearl laced pedestals
In the pungent underbelly of America
That are surmounted by shit
There's no room to breathe here
But we step in it knees deep
And *grow*
Because the struggle's just fertilizer

They wash us down
And
We are hyper visible when they need us
Yet made to be invisible and covered again
When they don't
We grow tired of being volleyed from your expectation
To being disappointed!

On behalf of many
Strong
      Black
            Women
I'll tell you this…
Sometimes, we don't *want* to be
Sometimes, I want to be vulnerable
Without the risk of being taken advantage of
Sometimes, I want to put my hand into a grip that firmer than mine
Sometimes, I want to be soft, and cry, and **free**
Of this trope
But I tread this path of thinking lightly
I haven't the luxury of resting to long
This armor is *heavy*
But necessary
So, I'm sorry. I cannot stay or relax here
As I'm already, preparing to battle again!

Once we've discovered the sound of our own voice,
it is even more critical to realize and enforce it's value.

When we know we deserve to be heard, we know we also deserve
to be seen.

We deserve to take up space.

Deep Throat

I know what you're thinking
I even bet, you'd like to find your way there
Putting yourself into her warm, moist, space
But it ain't that type of party
So, let's forgo all the pleasantries
Cause there'll be NO acquiescing to your whims
OR caressing your…ego
No matter how big you THINK it is
The only thing for you to get intimate with here?
Is this LESSON
And the title of the piece seemed so inviting, didn't it?

How disappointing for you to find
That the reward of an open orifice
Doesn't belong to you
That the soft of her flesh doesn't care to bend for you
Because the harsh reality of it all is
That a woman with an open throat, is a *threat*
In fact, she's more than that
More than dangerous
She, is determined
She is a defiant declaration dismantling the depths of disrespect
More than a disruption
She is a detonator ready to blow shit up
Did you really think you could contain her
Her belly a combustion chamber
When her diaphragm's inflated
Just before firing
An open throat? Is only but a cleared pathway
That funnels the explosion, you never saw coming
Not for lack of warning

But simply because, you, weren't even looking
You never care to listen
You're so comfortable in the discomfort of her of quiet
So you missed the internal rumblings of her awakening
Missed the bulging of her trachea shifting into bullhorn
Because from the moment she's born
She's taught to fade to black for men
And in doing so
She made silent sacrifice of her mind
Her speech
Her body
And *you* let her
Lay your ego out before her as alter
and have the nerve to look down on her as she falls to her knees
When you look down on a woman with the desire
to only gaze upon the top of her head
You do yourself no favors
She may kneel
But it is in pursuit of a different kind of gratification
Sometimes, even *she* is humbled by her *own* evolution
Pulling the proverbial phallus from her esophagus
She will breathe, and speak, and taste new things
Beyond what you've fed her
She sobers from Inebriated consciousness
She's done drinking your deceit
When a woman in this condition
Coughs up all your bullshit
It becomes fertilizer at her feet
Chemical laced toxicity transmuted into nutrient laden soil
It's how she remains grounded
Even when everything around her is wavering
She is *still*

Still here
Still growing
Still learning
She's been tilling her earth all this time
When the buck comes to call
When an informed woman comes to harvest
She reaps the reward from all the tears she sown into herself
Replenishing parts of her she thought lost forever
It becomes the persistence fueling her
As she presses back against subjugation

And at times, She grows weary
But remains steadfast in coming for EVERYTHING
That is equitably hers
You can tell her no 47 times
But it is her **supreme** right to **court** her dreams
And that's word to **Ketanji**
A woman with an open throat, has a voice
She will rebuke you *and* your secrets
No longer will she swallow and house your lies in her belly
Aborting your complacency
Daring to delineate the dichotomy of womanhood
Of being subhuman and superhero
Of being subservient and yet superior
She conjures all your *fears*
In the past you called them witches
But magical melanated beings be deity
Knows you'd love nothing more than to burn her
Because she knows what's at stake
And yet, keeps on fighting
They'd love to chalk it up to emotional complaining
'Oh, she's just nagging'

And you should know?
That is it no mild feat to keep an educated woman *silenced*
But it is necessary
Because how many *men* do *you* know
Have survived the heat of dragon's breath?!

And She possesses the word of fire to ignite a global movement
She bites back at all forms of oppression
ALL AT ONCE
There is no hierarchy of one's plight over the other
Let me tell you
Her self determination?
Could cost you, your life!

Cause She'll burn it all to ground and emerge covered in the ash
laced soot of those who tried to bury her
A woman who's released her throat chakra??
Sings a tune of *celebration*
Her *tongue* be the beating of tribal drums welcoming in a new era

She isn't born as
But over *time*
BECOMES a woman!
....and her throat?
Is DEEPER, than you THINK

Confidence is needed in part, to fuel our ambitions.
To pursue everything the world says we aren't good enough for.
To blaze a path forward in a male dominated society!

So…

This one's for the dreamers.
The ones still figuring it out, the ones who haven't learned how,
and for all the dreams cut short.

For the Dreamers

To quote our forever FLOTUS, Thee Michelle Obama
"The measure of any society, is in how it treats its women and
girls"
So, what does it say about US
The United States of America
Where you can be anything you aspire to be
Except respected. Valued. Heard.
Especially if you look, walk, or talk anything like me
Young, black, comfortable wielding my feminine energy
In this society you can dream of being anything
Except on par with the men who run it
Sure
Women can fetch your coffee
File your papers
Or even fall to our knees to satisfy
But some men get a lil dumbfounded
When they aren't the ones pulling the strings
Because to *them*
A woman looking anywhere above a man's waist line
Means, we've set our sights too high
So forgive me if I find it disillusioned to think
We shattered "that glass" a long time ago
That even with 18 million cracks
A great number of cis white men still sit behind that jawn
and laugh
Watching as we feverishly pound at its surface
But it's been reinforced many times over
Over centuries of time
Double paned
With an extra layering of male ego
Uhhh...It's pretty dammed thick

Granted
I can acknowledge that I have something
that many other women around the world lack
Access
Here I am
Still fighting in the same vein for equal treatment
As young girls in many cultures
are still fighting for
Being attacked and jailed for
Hell, many are still losing their *lives* for an education
Yet, here I stand
Residing in a nation where women of color
Are among the highest educated population and *still*
Find ourselves fighting for fair wages
that mirrors our male counterparts in the very same positions

Check this…
Black women working as physicians and surgeons?
Make just 54 cents for every dollar paid to white men
Guess they just keep raising the height of that there ceiling
OR rather it's akin to a glass enclosed basement
A sort of sad yet entertaining lower-level exhibit
Made up of all the women they've caged in
All the women who've given up or forgotten *how* to dream
All the women they've gotten to just stare at the pretty flowers
While they, *dream snatchers*
Click clack
cock back
and BLOW the ambitions out the BACK of their heads

Cause girls like Malala? Don't matter!
So what does it matter when a woman's brain in her head
doesn't refer to her intellect anyway?!

And the seed of a flower
Has no feelings that we know of
But it has purpose
It never concerns itself that it'll never get to grow or bloom
Or that the pot it's in, is too big or too small
Its only concern, is that it *will be* a flower
Perhaps, this is because
Power isn't something to be obtained outside ourselves
But from within
Fostered until we believe
And *then* unleashed
Understand
That **empowerment** is establishing that you're *worth* it
And then *acting* like it

So when does a woman get to dream?
Trick question…
She doesn't
She must remain woke
On guard and ready to defend at any given moment
Always pushing forward in pursuit of it
BUT
We aren't allowed to pursue our careers as aggressively as men
Tuh! NO
I won't stand still
In fact
I'll stride in confidence that a better futures' ahead

But I'mma *strut* in stilettos to juxtapose the idea
That I should *shrink* myself to appease all the short men in the
room

Who gives a damn how he feels!
The clickity clack of my heels is the sound of me more than breaking
But crushing generational curses
And gender normative standards

So forget my bottoms being that of blood red
The bottom of my soles is **black** like melanin
Because I stay pounding the pavement
I'm floating on every prayer my ancestors wove into their tears
That watered the earth each time they wept
So, close your eyes if you wish to see all the "pretty things"
But if you wish to see your dreams?
You must live with your eyes *open*
Cause when we as woman dare to more than sleep
But actively take action towards the vision
Young girls everywhere WAKE UP and *dare* to do the same
Give them MORE than the dream
Give them the reality

When it's real.

When it's right.

Love,

be like natural honey in my herbal tea on

a beautiful Sunday morning.

Butterflies & Coffee

He's like…
A shot of coffee right into the bellies of the butterflies in mine
They cha-cha alongside my excitement
Brushes up against my love
Grabs it by the hips and immerses it in heat
I didn't think the rush could get any quicker than this
But I feel *spirited*
Come alive with wonder
And I wonder if his butterflies are glowing…. like mine
Can they spot light the dance floor bright enough for you?
Have our shadows in tango
Flirting in tune too
Can they catch my rhythm the way you do?
Put a song in my grasp
While you grip
There's no cadence more fluid

Sprawled between these sheets
In our music
Lies you & I
the perfect 5th lives in the sound
found two-thirds along the way of you saying my name
We embrace along frequencies
hella beautiful
Fluttering amidst the intervals is my heart
Beating
Beating
Beating
Pull me into you
While I press you INto me

95

I want to sway in unison
Two step into eternity with you

Dip just below the baseline
Melt into your gaze

Can your eyes dance with my smile?
Choreograph moves worth learning?
Retrace my steps to the playback of your memory
Let your lips leave lyrics lilting in laughter
Putting lazy Sunday mornings on a loop
While
You teach me to perfectly play your soul sequence
I'll always be a willing student for you
Place your hand upon mine
Caress my wrist
Linger in your instruction
And strum the strings of my passion
Play me
Beautifully
Loudly
Play me
Beautifully
Loudly
On repeat
And in all the ways a woman like me deserves to be heard

Today
Let no funeral procession play
NOT today
Today
Let turning pages be whispered kisses
into the palms of black men
Let paperback be soft landing and
gentle push into the fold
In THIS moment
Let my love, this ode, this documented proof
be recycled affirmation
That you are respected
You are appreciated
You are necessary
YOU are crowned

In the Presence of Black Men

When a black man walks
My eyes light up
He saunters in with a distinguishable *swag*
That belongs to none other than the great. **Black.** Man.
Yeah, you may make the hairs on porcelain skin stand on end
But people often fear what they don't understand
Let's not pretend, to that end, they aren't envious
Even the ones claiming to be oblivious
Oh, they "don't see color"
But I see you **King** in *all* your glory
No matter how many short endings
Inconsistencies
Or outright fabrications
They attempt to add to your story
I see the truth in you
From the curl, kink, or loc of your hair
Or the subtle glow of that smooth bald head
To the spread of your nose
To the chisel of your jaw
To the *strength* of your hands
Etched into the depth of your melanin
King, I see the **GOD** in you
Higher authority resounds in the blessing of your voice
It is said the power of life and death resides at tip of one's tongue
So, when a black man speaks
My ears perk up
I'm ready. At attention. Just anticipating
Whatever a man with good sense is bringing to my mental table
Cause if he's able to educate, he's able to lead
No matter how impoverished his life
The black man is King of improvising

So, who better to understand where we lack, or what we need, and take that stand
Than our men?
Who better to mentor young misguided black boys than, our men?
There be resistance in his semantics speaking on strategies of protection against white antics
And YOU should be listening, every time
When he finds purpose in reaching down and pulling up the next
There is sacrifice on the kiss of a black man's lips
When his purpose is in pulling up the next
When he is focused on building
THAT my friends is more than care
So, when a black man loves
Kingdoms are risen and protected
Black women are protected
Black children are protected
Black businesses are protected
Black success is protected
Black wealth is instated and replicated
So that black **legacies** are protected!

So, when a black man is silent…
My heart is on alert and my arms lift up
The weight of loss battles lay upon his tongue
The blood of his brothers gurgles up in his throat
He is likely listening to the whispers of death upon his ears
While the weight of oppression sits upon his chest
Another obstruction of breath
As he wide eyed-ly looks for death at every passing corner
No longer does it lurk in the shadows
But it *brazenly* hunts him down in the brightness of day
Suddenly. Harshly. Violently.
and without MERCY

All in an *instant*!
Mission accomplished, IF death wins

So, when a black man is quiet
Find ways to soothe his fears
And carry him in the breadth of your prayers
Love him
Love him through his silence
When he is *most* impenetrable
Caress him in the soft of your **embrace**

There is an unappreciated
Underestimated
and often unspoken **fragility** in what it means to be a black man
So love him
Every time YOU are in his presence

There is an immeasurable admiration
for us
But no words
Well…none that are sufficient in my book.
(literally AND figuratively)

We make being "othered" look, dare I say, easy?
We make it beautiful and creative
We make it magical.
Black girl magic
Be declaration AND affirmation!
And yet, somehow, an understatement.

Black Goddess Magic

If the original Eve bore depths of melanin in her skin
Then it's fair to reason, that black women

Are the only beings who've ever given birth to <u>themselves</u>

Could you imagine?
Being tasked with such a *splendid* feat
Birthing a version of herself
Birthing, humanity

If that isn't evidence of **GOD**
...then
I don't know what is

Now
I'm not SAYING GOD is physical black woman

But we possess the qualities of one
Giving birth to black sons
Like the blackness of the sky gives *life* to the SUN
The planets
The galaxies
Every entity of light
Can all be seen
…in the *space* of the darkness

When the black woman emerged
The entire atmosphere stood agape
In the bluest of midnight

A creation so *powerful* she breached the sky
Stepping out from the heavens
Glow of her skin, dusted in stars

She IS a STAR

Far removed
Or
Too distant
Burning too hot
And too *magnificent* to be contained

I said
SHE
Is far removed from the bullshit
Purposefully distant
From all the broken versions of herself
Burning too hot in all her glory
For negative vibes to penetrate her aura
And to gahhhh dayum magnanimous
to be *put* in anyone's box!

Now
I'm not saying the physical black woman is God
Just that she carries the essence of one
From her **crown** to her hips
When the next being of divinity emerges
She will hold 'em in her holy
Imprint unperverted scripture
Upon his forehead with the kiss of her lips
So that
This time
They may remember, from whence they came

She will gift 'em the heavens
And every child will know
That they can find redemption and rebirth
At
Their **mother's** feet

Dear Melanin,

My love and appreciation run deep.
Rooted in every letter of the color that
wraps itself around my skin.
This divinity hums freedom songs in every shade
that we are found in.
We, just have to learn how to listen.
Learn the lyrics and sing them in every key of our healing.
Maybe even one day, "they" will learn to listen to.
For, vying to sing in harmony
As opposed to wreaking havoc
is a *blessing*.
PEACE is a gift black America bestows on its oppressor
Everyday!
And this is made possible,
only
by the power of black love.

ABOUT THE AUTHOR

Born and raised in Philadelphia, Vee is poetically known as Lady Syren. A pen name and spiritual embodiment of both her feminine essence, and the fire she exudes wile executing her passions. Not only using her work as a fitness instructor, writer, and performer as a personal means of education, therapy, and healing. But also, as a vehicle to propel forward a positive image, narrative, and deep love for blackness, with a specific focus on black women. She is a proud member of the African National Women's Organization, and has been featured on many platforms promoting advocacy for women in general.
Be sure to follow her and look out for future projects and events on Instagram @LadySyren